50 Global Flavors Taco Recipes

By: Kelly Johnson

Table of Contents

- Korean Bulgogi Beef Tacos
- Thai Peanut Chicken Tacos
- Indian Butter Chicken Tacos
- Moroccan Lamb Tacos
- Japanese Teriyaki Salmon Tacos
- Greek Gyro Tacos with Tzatziki
- Mexican Mole Chicken Tacos
- Cajun Shrimp Tacos
- Cuban Mojo Pork Tacos
- Vietnamese Banh Mi Tacos
- Jamaican Jerk Chicken Tacos
- Italian Meatball Marinara Tacos
- Argentine Chimichurri Steak Tacos
- Chinese Peking Duck Tacos
- Filipino Adobo Pork Tacos
- Lebanese Falafel Tacos
- Ethiopian Berbere Chicken Tacos
- Peruvian Ceviche Tacos
- Brazilian Feijoada Tacos
- Swedish Meatball Tacos
- French Ratatouille Tacos
- German Bratwurst Tacos
- Spanish Paella Tacos
- Turkish Kebab Tacos
- Indonesian Satay Chicken Tacos
- Russian Beef Stroganoff Tacos
- Hawaiian Ahi Poke Tacos
- Nigerian Suya Beef Tacos
- Swiss Fondue Cheese Tacos
- Israeli Shakshuka Tacos
- Malaysian Curry Chicken Tacos
- Chilean Empanada Tacos
- Australian BBQ Kangaroo Tacos
- Saudi Arabian Shawarma Tacos
- Portuguese Piri-Piri Chicken Tacos
- South African Bobotie Tacos

- Caribbean Curry Goat Tacos
- Polish Pierogi Tacos
- Moroccan Harissa Veggie Tacos
- Egyptian Koshari Tacos
- Korean Kimchi Pork Belly Tacos
- Mexican Al Pastor Tacos
- Dominican Mangu Tacos
- Venezuelan Arepa Tacos
- Thai Green Curry Fish Tacos
- Italian Caprese Tacos
- Indian Tandoori Paneer Tacos
- Pakistani Nihari Beef Tacos
- Colombian Ajiaco Chicken Tacos
- Singaporean Chili Crab Tacos

Korean Bulgogi Beef Tacos

Ingredients

For the Bulgogi Beef:

- 1 lb (450g) beef ribeye or sirloin, thinly sliced
- 3 tbsp soy sauce
- 1 tbsp sesame oil
- 1 tbsp brown sugar
- 2 cloves garlic, minced
- 1 tbsp grated ginger
- 1 tbsp gochujang (Korean chili paste)
- 1 tsp rice vinegar
- 1 pear (or apple), grated (optional, for tenderizing)
- 2 green onions, chopped
- 1 tbsp sesame seeds
- 1 tbsp vegetable oil

For the Tacos:

- 8 small tortillas (flour or corn)
- 1 cup kimchi, chopped
- ½ cup shredded cabbage or slaw mix
- ¼ cup sliced radishes
- 2 tbsp chopped cilantro
- Lime wedges

Optional Sauce:

- ¼ cup mayo
- 1 tbsp gochujang
- 1 tsp lime juice

Instructions

1. Marinate the Beef

- In a bowl, mix soy sauce, sesame oil, brown sugar, garlic, ginger, gochujang, rice vinegar, grated pear, and green onions.
- Add the thinly sliced beef and stir to coat evenly. Cover and refrigerate for at least 30 minutes or overnight.

2. Cook the Beef

- Heat vegetable oil in a skillet over medium-high heat. Cook the marinated beef in batches to avoid overcrowding, 2-3 minutes per side, until browned and cooked through. Sprinkle with sesame seeds while cooking.

3. Assemble the Tacos

- Warm the tortillas on a pan or over a flame.
- Fill each tortilla with a generous serving of bulgogi beef.
- Top with chopped kimchi, shredded cabbage, radishes, and cilantro.

4. Add Sauce (Optional)

- Mix mayo, gochujang, and lime juice in a small bowl. Drizzle over the tacos for added flavor.

5. Serve

- Serve with lime wedges on the side and enjoy the fusion of Korean and Mexican flavors!

Thai Peanut Chicken Tacos

Ingredients

For the Chicken:

- 1 lb (450g) chicken thighs or breasts, thinly sliced
- 2 tbsp soy sauce
- 1 tbsp sesame oil
- 2 cloves garlic, minced
- 1 tbsp ginger, minced
- 1 tbsp lime juice

For the Peanut Sauce:

- 1/2 cup creamy peanut butter
- 2 tbsp soy sauce
- 1 tbsp lime juice
- 1 tbsp honey or maple syrup
- 1-2 tbsp water (to thin)
- 1 tsp sriracha (optional)

For the Tacos:

- 8 small tortillas
- 1 cup shredded cabbage
- 1/2 cup shredded carrots
- 1/4 cup chopped cilantro
- Lime wedges for serving

Instructions

1. **Marinate the Chicken:** In a bowl, combine chicken, soy sauce, sesame oil, garlic, ginger, and lime juice. Marinate for at least 30 minutes.
2. **Cook the Chicken:** Heat a skillet over medium-high heat and cook the marinated chicken until cooked through, about 5-7 minutes.
3. **Make the Peanut Sauce:** In a bowl, mix peanut butter, soy sauce, lime juice, honey, and water until smooth. Adjust consistency with more water if needed.
4. **Assemble the Tacos:** Warm tortillas, fill with chicken, and top with cabbage, carrots, and cilantro. Drizzle with peanut sauce.
5. **Serve:** Enjoy with lime wedges!

Indian Butter Chicken Tacos

Ingredients

For the Butter Chicken:

- 1 lb (450g) chicken thighs or breasts, diced
- 1 tbsp vegetable oil
- 1 onion, finely chopped
- 2 cloves garlic, minced
- 1 tbsp ginger, minced
- 1 tbsp garam masala
- 1 tsp turmeric
- 1 tsp cumin
- 1 cup canned crushed tomatoes
- 1/2 cup heavy cream
- Salt to taste

For the Tacos:

- 8 small tortillas
- Fresh cilantro, chopped
- Sliced jalapeños (optional)
- Lime wedges for serving

Instructions

1. **Cook the Chicken:** Heat oil in a pan over medium heat. Add onion, garlic, and ginger; sauté until softened.
2. **Add Spices and Chicken:** Stir in garam masala, turmeric, and cumin. Add chicken and cook until browned.
3. **Make the Sauce:** Add crushed tomatoes and simmer for 15 minutes. Stir in cream and season with salt.
4. **Assemble the Tacos:** Warm tortillas and fill with butter chicken. Top with cilantro and jalapeños.
5. **Serve:** Enjoy with lime wedges!

Moroccan Lamb Tacos

Ingredients

For the Lamb:

- 1 lb (450g) ground lamb
- 1 onion, finely chopped
- 2 cloves garlic, minced
- 1 tbsp ground cumin
- 1 tbsp ground coriander
- 1 tsp cinnamon
- 1/2 tsp cayenne pepper (optional)
- Salt and pepper to taste

For the Tacos:

- 8 small tortillas
- 1 cup tzatziki sauce or yogurt
- 1 cup diced cucumbers
- 1/2 cup chopped fresh mint
- Lime wedges for serving

Instructions

1. **Cook the Lamb:** In a skillet over medium heat, sauté onion and garlic until soft. Add ground lamb and cook until browned. Stir in spices and season with salt and pepper.
2. **Assemble the Tacos:** Warm tortillas, fill with lamb mixture, and top with tzatziki, cucumbers, and mint.
3. **Serve:** Enjoy with lime wedges!

Japanese Teriyaki Salmon Tacos

Ingredients

For the Salmon:

- 1 lb (450g) salmon fillets
- 1/4 cup teriyaki sauce
- 1 tbsp sesame oil

For the Tacos:

- 8 small tortillas
- 1 cup shredded cabbage
- 1/2 cup sliced green onions
- 1/4 cup chopped cilantro
- Lime wedges for serving

Instructions

1. **Marinate the Salmon:** In a bowl, coat the salmon fillets with teriyaki sauce and sesame oil. Let marinate for at least 15 minutes.
2. **Cook the Salmon:** Heat a grill or skillet over medium heat and cook the salmon for about 4-5 minutes per side or until cooked through.
3. **Assemble the Tacos:** Warm tortillas and fill with salmon, cabbage, green onions, and cilantro.
4. **Serve:** Enjoy with lime wedges!

Greek Gyro Tacos with Tzatziki

Ingredients

For the Gyro:

- 1 lb (450g) ground lamb or beef
- 1 onion, finely chopped
- 2 cloves garlic, minced
- 1 tbsp dried oregano
- 1 tsp cumin
- Salt and pepper to taste

For the Tzatziki Sauce:

- 1 cup Greek yogurt
- 1/2 cucumber, grated and drained
- 1 clove garlic, minced
- 1 tbsp olive oil
- 1 tbsp lemon juice
- Salt to taste

For the Tacos:

- 8 small tortillas
- Sliced tomatoes
- Sliced red onion
- Fresh parsley, chopped

Instructions

1. **Cook the Gyro Meat:** In a skillet, cook onion and garlic until soft. Add ground meat, oregano, cumin, salt, and pepper, cooking until browned.
2. **Make the Tzatziki:** In a bowl, mix yogurt, cucumber, garlic, olive oil, lemon juice, and salt.
3. **Assemble the Tacos:** Warm tortillas, fill with gyro meat, tomatoes, red onion, and parsley. Drizzle with tzatziki.
4. **Serve:** Enjoy!

Mexican Mole Chicken Tacos

Ingredients

For the Mole Chicken:

- 1 lb (450g) chicken thighs, cooked and shredded
- 1/2 cup mole sauce (store-bought or homemade)
- 1/4 cup chicken broth

For the Tacos:

- 8 small tortillas
- 1 cup chopped lettuce
- 1/2 cup crumbled queso fresco
- Avocado slices
- Lime wedges for serving

Instructions

1. **Prepare the Mole Chicken:** In a pan, combine shredded chicken, mole sauce, and chicken broth. Simmer until heated through.
2. **Assemble the Tacos:** Warm tortillas, fill with mole chicken, lettuce, queso fresco, and avocado.
3. **Serve:** Enjoy with lime wedges!

Cajun Shrimp Tacos

Ingredients

For the Shrimp:

- 1 lb (450g) shrimp, peeled and deveined
- 1 tbsp Cajun seasoning
- 1 tbsp olive oil

For the Tacos:

- 8 small tortillas
- 1 cup shredded cabbage
- 1/2 cup diced tomatoes
- 1/4 cup chopped green onions
- Lime wedges for serving

Instructions

1. **Season and Cook the Shrimp:** Toss shrimp with Cajun seasoning and olive oil. Cook in a skillet over medium heat until pink and cooked through, about 3-4 minutes.
2. **Assemble the Tacos:** Warm tortillas, fill with shrimp, cabbage, tomatoes, and green onions.
3. **Serve:** Enjoy with lime wedges!

Cuban Mojo Pork Tacos

Ingredients

For the Mojo Pork:

- 1 lb (450g) pork shoulder, cooked and shredded
- 1/4 cup mojo sauce (citrus marinade)

For the Tacos:

- 8 small tortillas
- 1 cup diced avocado
- 1/2 cup chopped cilantro
- Lime wedges for serving

Instructions

1. **Prepare the Mojo Pork:** In a bowl, mix shredded pork with mojo sauce until well coated.
2. **Assemble the Tacos:** Warm tortillas, fill with mojo pork, avocado, and cilantro.
3. **Serve:** Enjoy with lime wedges!

Vietnamese Banh Mi Tacos

Ingredients

For the Pork:

- 1 lb (450g) pork tenderloin, thinly sliced
- 2 tbsp soy sauce
- 1 tbsp fish sauce
- 1 tbsp sugar

For the Pickled Vegetables:

- 1/2 cup carrots, julienned
- 1/2 cup daikon radish, julienned
- 1/4 cup rice vinegar
- 1/4 cup sugar
- 1/4 cup water

For the Tacos:

- 8 small tortillas
- Fresh cilantro
- Sliced jalapeños
- Lime wedges for serving

Instructions

1. **Marinate the Pork:** Combine pork, soy sauce, fish sauce, and sugar in a bowl. Marinate for at least 30 minutes.
2. **Pickle the Vegetables:** In a bowl, mix carrots, daikon, rice vinegar, sugar, and water. Let sit for at least 30 minutes.
3. **Cook the Pork:** Heat a skillet over medium heat and cook marinated pork until cooked through.
4. **Assemble the Tacos:** Warm tortillas, fill with pork, pickled vegetables, cilantro, and jalapeños.
5. **Serve:** Enjoy with lime wedges!

Jamaican Jerk Chicken Tacos

Ingredients

For the Jerk Chicken:

- 1 lb (450g) chicken thighs or breasts, diced
- 2 tbsp jerk seasoning
- 1 tbsp olive oil

For the Tacos:

- 8 small tortillas
- 1 cup shredded lettuce
- 1/2 cup diced mango
- 1/4 cup chopped cilantro
- Lime wedges for serving

Instructions

1. **Marinate the Chicken:** Toss chicken with jerk seasoning and olive oil. Let marinate for at least 30 minutes.
2. **Cook the Chicken:** Heat a skillet over medium heat and cook chicken until browned and cooked through.
3. **Assemble the Tacos:** Warm tortillas, fill with jerk chicken, lettuce, mango, and cilantro.
4. **Serve:** Enjoy with lime wedges!

Italian Meatball Marinara Tacos

Ingredients

For the Meatballs:

- 1 lb (450g) ground beef or turkey
- 1/4 cup breadcrumbs
- 1/4 cup grated Parmesan cheese
- 1 egg
- 2 cloves garlic, minced
- 1 tsp Italian seasoning
- Salt and pepper to taste

For the Marinara:

- 1 cup marinara sauce

For the Tacos:

- 8 small tortillas
- Shredded mozzarella cheese
- Fresh basil, chopped

Instructions

1. **Make the Meatballs:** In a bowl, combine all meatball ingredients and mix. Form into small meatballs.
2. **Cook the Meatballs:** In a skillet, cook meatballs until browned and cooked through. Add marinara sauce and simmer for 5 minutes.
3. **Assemble the Tacos:** Warm tortillas, fill with meatballs and sauce, and top with mozzarella and basil.
4. **Serve:** Enjoy!

Argentine Chimichurri Steak Tacos

Ingredients

For the Steak:

- 1 lb (450g) flank steak
- Salt and pepper to taste
- 1 tbsp olive oil

For the Chimichurri Sauce:

- 1/2 cup fresh parsley, chopped
- 1/4 cup fresh oregano, chopped
- 4 cloves garlic, minced
- 1/2 cup olive oil
- 2 tbsp red wine vinegar
- Salt and pepper to taste

For the Tacos:

- 8 small tortillas
- Sliced avocado
- Sliced radishes

Instructions

1. **Cook the Steak:** Season flank steak with salt and pepper. Heat olive oil in a skillet over medium-high heat and cook steak for 5-7 minutes per side or until desired doneness. Let rest, then slice thinly.
2. **Make the Chimichurri:** In a bowl, mix parsley, oregano, garlic, olive oil, vinegar, salt, and pepper.
3. **Assemble the Tacos:** Warm tortillas, fill with sliced steak, chimichurri, avocado, and radishes.
4. **Serve:** Enjoy!

Chinese Peking Duck Tacos

Ingredients

For the Peking Duck:

- 1 lb (450g) Peking duck (store-bought or homemade)
- 1/4 cup hoisin sauce
- 1/4 cup green onions, sliced

For the Tacos:

- 8 small tortillas
- Sliced cucumbers
- Fresh cilantro

Instructions

1. **Prepare the Duck:** If using store-bought Peking duck, heat according to package instructions.
2. **Assemble the Tacos:** Warm tortillas, fill with duck, hoisin sauce, green onions, cucumbers, and cilantro.
3. **Serve:** Enjoy!

Filipino Adobo Pork Tacos

Ingredients

For the Adobo Pork:

- 1 lb (450g) pork shoulder, cubed
- 1/2 cup soy sauce
- 1/2 cup vinegar
- 4 cloves garlic, minced
- 2 bay leaves
- 1 tsp black peppercorns

For the Tacos:

- 8 small tortillas
- Sliced green onions
- Chopped cilantro

Instructions

1. **Cook the Adobo Pork:** In a pot, combine pork, soy sauce, vinegar, garlic, bay leaves, and peppercorns. Simmer until pork is tender, about 1.5 hours.
2. **Shred the Pork:** Remove bay leaves and shred the pork.
3. **Assemble the Tacos:** Warm tortillas, fill with adobo pork, and top with green onions and cilantro.
4. **Serve:** Enjoy!

Lebanese Falafel Tacos

Ingredients

For the Falafel:

- 1 can (15 oz) chickpeas, drained
- 1/4 cup onion, chopped
- 2 cloves garlic, minced
- 1/4 cup parsley, chopped
- 1 tsp cumin
- 1 tsp coriander
- Salt and pepper to taste
- Oil for frying

For the Tacos:

- 8 small tortillas
- Tzatziki or tahini sauce
- Shredded lettuce
- Diced tomatoes

Instructions

1. **Make the Falafel Mixture:** In a food processor, blend chickpeas, onion, garlic, parsley, cumin, coriander, salt, and pepper until coarse.
2. **Form and Fry Falafel:** Form into balls and fry in hot oil until golden brown.
3. **Assemble the Tacos:** Warm tortillas, fill with falafel, tzatziki, lettuce, and tomatoes.
4. **Serve:** Enjoy!

Ethiopian Berbere Chicken Tacos

Ingredients

For the Chicken:

- 1 lb (450g) chicken thighs, diced
- 2 tbsp berbere spice mix
- 1 tbsp olive oil

For the Tacos:

- 8 small tortillas
- 1 cup shredded cabbage
- 1/2 cup diced tomatoes
- Chopped fresh cilantro

Instructions

1. **Cook the Chicken:** Toss chicken with berbere spice and olive oil. Cook in a skillet over medium heat until cooked through, about 7-10 minutes.
2. **Assemble the Tacos:** Warm tortillas, fill with chicken, cabbage, tomatoes, and cilantro.
3. **Serve:** Enjoy!

Peruvian Ceviche Tacos

Ingredients

For the Ceviche:

- 1 lb (450g) fresh white fish (like tilapia), diced
- 1/2 cup lime juice
- 1/4 cup red onion, thinly sliced
- 1 jalapeño, minced
- 1/4 cup cilantro, chopped
- Salt to taste

For the Tacos:

- 8 small tortillas
- Avocado slices
- Lime wedges for serving

Instructions

1. **Prepare the Ceviche:** In a bowl, combine fish, lime juice, red onion, jalapeño, cilantro, and salt. Let marinate for 15-20 minutes.
2. **Assemble the Tacos:** Warm tortillas, fill with ceviche, and top with avocado.
3. **Serve:** Enjoy with lime wedges!

Brazilian Feijoada Tacos

Ingredients

For the Feijoada:

- 1 lb (450g) black beans, cooked
- 1/2 lb (225g) pork sausage, sliced
- 1/2 lb (225g) smoked ham, diced
- 1 onion, chopped
- 2 cloves garlic, minced
- 2 cups chicken broth
- Salt and pepper to taste

For the Tacos:

- 8 small tortillas
- Sliced oranges
- Fresh cilantro

Instructions

1. **Cook the Feijoada:** In a pot, sauté onion and garlic until soft. Add sausage, ham, black beans, and chicken broth. Simmer for 30 minutes, seasoning with salt and pepper.
2. **Assemble the Tacos:** Warm tortillas, fill with feijoada, and top with orange slices and cilantro.
3. **Serve:** Enjoy!

Swedish Meatball Tacos

Ingredients

For the Meatballs:

- 1 lb (450g) ground beef
- 1/4 cup breadcrumbs
- 1/4 cup grated onion
- 1 egg
- 1 tsp allspice
- Salt and pepper to taste

For the Gravy:

- 1 cup beef broth
- 1/2 cup heavy cream
- 1 tbsp Worcestershire sauce

For the Tacos:

- 8 small tortillas
- Lingonberry sauce (optional)
- Fresh parsley, chopped

Instructions

1. **Make the Meatballs:** In a bowl, mix all meatball ingredients and form into small balls.
2. **Cook the Meatballs:** In a skillet, cook meatballs until browned and cooked through. Remove and set aside.
3. **Make the Gravy:** In the same skillet, add broth, cream, and Worcestershire sauce. Simmer until thickened.
4. **Assemble the Tacos:** Warm tortillas, fill with meatballs, drizzle with gravy, and top with lingonberry sauce and parsley.
5. **Serve:** Enjoy!

French Ratatouille Tacos

Ingredients

For the Ratatouille:

- 1 medium eggplant, diced
- 1 zucchini, diced
- 1 bell pepper, diced
- 1 onion, chopped
- 2 cloves garlic, minced
- 1 can (14 oz) diced tomatoes
- 2 tbsp olive oil
- Salt and pepper to taste
- 1 tsp dried herbs (thyme, basil, or oregano)

For the Tacos:

- 8 small tortillas
- Crumbled feta cheese
- Fresh basil leaves

Instructions

1. **Cook the Ratatouille:** In a skillet, heat olive oil over medium heat. Sauté onion and garlic until translucent. Add eggplant, zucchini, and bell pepper; cook until softened. Stir in diced tomatoes, herbs, salt, and pepper. Simmer for 15-20 minutes.
2. **Assemble the Tacos:** Warm tortillas, fill with ratatouille, and top with feta cheese and fresh basil.
3. **Serve:** Enjoy!

German Bratwurst Tacos

Ingredients

For the Bratwurst:

- 1 lb (450g) bratwurst sausages
- 1 onion, sliced
- 1 tbsp mustard

For the Tacos:

- 8 small tortillas
- Sauerkraut
- Sliced pickles
- Chopped fresh parsley

Instructions

1. **Cook the Bratwurst:** Grill or pan-fry bratwurst until cooked through. Remove and let rest, then slice.
2. **Sauté the Onions:** In the same pan, sauté onions until caramelized.
3. **Assemble the Tacos:** Warm tortillas, fill with sliced bratwurst, sautéed onions, sauerkraut, pickles, and parsley.
4. **Serve:** Enjoy!

Spanish Paella Tacos

Ingredients

For the Paella Filling:

- 1 cup Arborio rice
- 2 cups chicken broth
- 1/2 lb (225g) shrimp, peeled and deveined
- 1/2 lb (225g) chicken thighs, diced
- 1/2 bell pepper, diced
- 1/2 onion, chopped
- 2 cloves garlic, minced
- 1 tsp smoked paprika
- 1/2 tsp saffron (optional)
- Olive oil
- Salt and pepper to taste

For the Tacos:

- 8 small tortillas
- Lemon wedges
- Fresh parsley, chopped

Instructions

1. **Cook the Paella Filling:** In a skillet, heat olive oil over medium heat. Sauté onion and garlic until soft. Add chicken and cook until browned. Stir in rice, broth, shrimp, bell pepper, paprika, saffron, salt, and pepper. Simmer until rice is tender, about 20 minutes.
2. **Assemble the Tacos:** Warm tortillas, fill with paella mixture, and top with parsley.
3. **Serve:** Enjoy with lemon wedges!

Turkish Kebab Tacos

Ingredients

For the Kebabs:

- 1 lb (450g) ground lamb or beef
- 1 onion, grated
- 2 cloves garlic, minced
- 1 tsp cumin
- 1 tsp paprika
- Salt and pepper to taste
- Skewers

For the Tacos:

- 8 small tortillas
- Sliced cucumbers
- Chopped tomatoes
- Fresh parsley
- Yogurt sauce (optional)

Instructions

1. **Make the Kebab Mixture:** In a bowl, combine ground meat, onion, garlic, cumin, paprika, salt, and pepper. Form into skewers.
2. **Grill the Kebabs:** Grill skewers on medium heat until cooked through.
3. **Assemble the Tacos:** Warm tortillas, fill with kebabs, cucumbers, tomatoes, and parsley. Drizzle with yogurt sauce if desired.
4. **Serve:** Enjoy!

Indonesian Satay Chicken Tacos

Ingredients

For the Satay Chicken:

- 1 lb (450g) chicken breast, cubed
- 1/4 cup soy sauce
- 1/4 cup peanut butter
- 2 tbsp honey
- 2 cloves garlic, minced
- 1 tsp ginger, grated

For the Tacos:

- 8 small tortillas
- Shredded cabbage
- Chopped peanuts
- Fresh cilantro

Instructions

1. **Make the Marinade:** In a bowl, whisk together soy sauce, peanut butter, honey, garlic, and ginger. Marinate chicken for at least 30 minutes.
2. **Cook the Chicken:** Thread marinated chicken onto skewers and grill until cooked through.
3. **Assemble the Tacos:** Warm tortillas, fill with satay chicken, cabbage, chopped peanuts, and cilantro.
4. **Serve:** Enjoy!

Russian Beef Stroganoff Tacos

Ingredients

For the Beef Stroganoff:

- 1 lb (450g) beef sirloin, thinly sliced
- 1 onion, sliced
- 2 cups mushrooms, sliced
- 2 cups beef broth
- 1 cup sour cream
- 2 tbsp flour
- Salt and pepper to taste
- Olive oil

For the Tacos:

- 8 small tortillas
- Fresh parsley, chopped

Instructions

1. **Cook the Beef:** In a skillet, heat olive oil over medium-high heat. Sauté beef until browned, then remove.
2. **Sauté the Vegetables:** In the same skillet, add onion and mushrooms; cook until softened. Stir in flour, then add beef broth and simmer until thickened. Return beef and stir in sour cream; season with salt and pepper.
3. **Assemble the Tacos:** Warm tortillas, fill with stroganoff mixture, and top with parsley.
4. **Serve:** Enjoy!

Hawaiian Ahi Poke Tacos

Ingredients

For the Ahi Poke:

- 1 lb (450g) sushi-grade ahi tuna, diced
- 1/4 cup soy sauce
- 1 tbsp sesame oil
- 1 green onion, chopped
- 1 tsp grated ginger
- 1 tbsp sesame seeds

For the Tacos:

- 8 small tortillas
- Sliced avocado
- Shredded cabbage

Instructions

1. **Make the Ahi Poke:** In a bowl, combine diced tuna, soy sauce, sesame oil, green onion, ginger, and sesame seeds.
2. **Assemble the Tacos:** Warm tortillas, fill with ahi poke, avocado, and cabbage.
3. **Serve:** Enjoy!

Nigerian Suya Beef Tacos

Ingredients

For the Suya Beef:

- 1 lb (450g) beef, thinly sliced
- 2 tbsp suya spice mix (or a blend of ground peanuts, paprika, cayenne, garlic powder, and salt)
- 2 tbsp vegetable oil

For the Tacos:

- 8 small tortillas
- Sliced tomatoes
- Chopped onions
- Shredded lettuce

Instructions

1. **Marinate the Beef:** In a bowl, toss beef with suya spice mix and oil. Marinate for at least 30 minutes.
2. **Cook the Beef:** Grill or pan-fry beef slices until cooked through.
3. **Assemble the Tacos:** Warm tortillas, fill with suya beef, tomatoes, onions, and lettuce.
4. **Serve:** Enjoy!

Swiss Fondue Cheese Tacos

Ingredients

For the Fondue Cheese:

- 1 cup Gruyère cheese, shredded
- 1 cup Emmental cheese, shredded
- 1 cup dry white wine
- 1 clove garlic, minced
- 1 tbsp cornstarch
- 1 tbsp lemon juice
- Freshly cracked black pepper

For the Tacos:

- 8 small tortillas
- Chopped chives

Instructions

1. **Prepare the Fondue:** In a saucepan, heat wine and garlic over medium heat until simmering. Gradually add cheeses, stirring until melted and smooth. Mix cornstarch with lemon juice, then stir into the cheese mixture. Season with pepper.
2. **Assemble the Tacos:** Warm tortillas, fill with cheese fondue, and sprinkle with chives.
3. **Serve:** Enjoy!

Israeli Shakshuka Tacos

Ingredients

For the Shakshuka:

- 1 tbsp olive oil
- 1 onion, chopped
- 1 bell pepper, chopped
- 2 cloves garlic, minced
- 1 can (14 oz) diced tomatoes
- 1 tsp cumin
- 1 tsp paprika
- Salt and pepper to taste
- 4 large eggs
- Fresh parsley, chopped

For the Tacos:

- 8 small tortillas
- Crumbled feta cheese

Instructions

1. **Cook the Shakshuka:** In a skillet, heat olive oil over medium heat. Sauté onion and bell pepper until soft. Add garlic, tomatoes, cumin, paprika, salt, and pepper. Simmer for 10 minutes.
2. **Add the Eggs:** Make wells in the mixture and crack an egg into each. Cover and cook until eggs are set.
3. **Assemble the Tacos:** Warm tortillas, fill with shakshuka, and top with feta and parsley.
4. **Serve:** Enjoy!

Malaysian Curry Chicken Tacos

Ingredients

For the Curry Chicken:

- 1 lb (450g) chicken breast, diced
- 1 onion, chopped
- 2 cloves garlic, minced
- 2 tbsp curry powder
- 1 can (14 oz) coconut milk
- Salt to taste

For the Tacos:

- 8 small tortillas
- Sliced cucumbers
- Chopped cilantro

Instructions

1. **Cook the Curry Chicken:** In a skillet, sauté onion and garlic until fragrant. Add chicken and cook until browned. Stir in curry powder and coconut milk; simmer for 15-20 minutes. Season with salt.
2. **Assemble the Tacos:** Warm tortillas, fill with curry chicken, cucumbers, and cilantro.
3. **Serve:** Enjoy!

Chilean Empanada Tacos

Ingredients

For the Filling:

- 1 lb (450g) ground beef
- 1 onion, chopped
- 2 cloves garlic, minced
- 1/2 cup olives, chopped
- 1/2 cup hard-boiled eggs, chopped
- 1 tsp cumin
- Salt and pepper to taste

For the Tacos:

- 8 small tortillas
- Chopped fresh parsley

Instructions

1. **Prepare the Filling:** In a skillet, cook onion and garlic until soft. Add ground beef, cumin, salt, and pepper; cook until browned. Stir in olives and hard-boiled eggs.
2. **Assemble the Tacos:** Warm tortillas, fill with the empanada filling, and top with parsley.
3. **Serve:** Enjoy!

Australian BBQ Kangaroo Tacos

Ingredients

For the Kangaroo Filling:

- 1 lb (450g) kangaroo fillet, thinly sliced
- 2 tbsp BBQ sauce
- Salt and pepper to taste

For the Tacos:

- 8 small tortillas
- Sliced avocado
- Shredded lettuce

Instructions

1. **Cook the Kangaroo:** In a skillet, heat BBQ sauce over medium heat. Add kangaroo slices, seasoning with salt and pepper, and cook until browned.
2. **Assemble the Tacos:** Warm tortillas, fill with kangaroo, avocado, and lettuce.
3. **Serve:** Enjoy!

Saudi Arabian Shawarma Tacos

Ingredients

For the Shawarma:

- 1 lb (450g) chicken or beef, thinly sliced
- 2 tbsp shawarma spice mix (cumin, coriander, paprika, garlic powder)
- 2 tbsp olive oil
- Salt to taste

For the Tacos:

- 8 small tortillas
- Sliced tomatoes
- Sliced onions
- Tahini sauce

Instructions

1. **Cook the Shawarma:** In a skillet, heat olive oil over medium heat. Add meat, shawarma spice mix, and salt; cook until browned and cooked through.
2. **Assemble the Tacos:** Warm tortillas, fill with shawarma, tomatoes, and onions. Drizzle with tahini sauce.
3. **Serve:** Enjoy!

Portuguese Piri-Piri Chicken Tacos

Ingredients

For the Piri-Piri Chicken:

- 1 lb (450g) chicken thighs, boneless and skinless
- 2 tbsp piri-piri sauce
- 1 tbsp olive oil

For the Tacos:

- 8 small tortillas
- Shredded cabbage
- Sliced radishes

Instructions

1. **Marinate the Chicken:** In a bowl, combine chicken, piri-piri sauce, and olive oil. Marinate for at least 30 minutes.
2. **Cook the Chicken:** Grill or pan-fry chicken until cooked through.
3. **Assemble the Tacos:** Warm tortillas, fill with piri-piri chicken, cabbage, and radishes.
4. **Serve:** Enjoy!

South African Bobotie Tacos

Ingredients

For the Bobotie Filling:

- 1 lb (450g) ground beef or lamb
- 1 onion, chopped
- 2 cloves garlic, minced
- 1/2 cup raisins
- 2 tbsp curry powder
- 1/2 cup milk
- 1 egg
- Salt and pepper to taste

For the Tacos:

- 8 small tortillas
- Chopped fresh coriander

Instructions

1. **Cook the Bobotie Filling:** In a skillet, cook onion and garlic until soft. Add ground meat, curry powder, salt, and pepper; cook until browned. Stir in raisins.
2. **Prepare the Custard Topping:** In a bowl, whisk together milk and egg; pour over the meat mixture. Bake at 350°F (175°C) for 20-25 minutes until set.
3. **Assemble the Tacos:** Warm tortillas, fill with bobotie filling, and top with coriander.
4. **Serve:** Enjoy!

Caribbean Curry Goat Tacos

Ingredients

For the Curry Goat Filling:

- 1 lb (450g) goat meat, diced
- 2 tbsp curry powder
- 1 onion, chopped
- 2 cloves garlic, minced
- 1 can (14 oz) coconut milk
- Salt and pepper to taste

For the Tacos:

- 8 small tortillas
- Chopped fresh cilantro
- Lime wedges

Instructions

1. **Cook the Goat:** In a pot, heat oil and sauté onion and garlic until fragrant. Add goat meat and curry powder; brown for a few minutes. Pour in coconut milk, season with salt and pepper, and simmer for 1-1.5 hours until tender.
2. **Assemble the Tacos:** Warm tortillas, fill with curry goat, and top with cilantro. Serve with lime wedges.
3. **Serve:** Enjoy!

Polish Pierogi Tacos

Ingredients

For the Filling:

- 1 lb (450g) potatoes, peeled and diced
- 1 cup cottage cheese
- 1 onion, chopped
- 2 tbsp butter
- Salt and pepper to taste

For the Tacos:

- 8 small tortillas
- Sour cream
- Chopped chives

Instructions

1. **Make the Filling:** Boil potatoes until tender; mash and mix with cottage cheese. In a skillet, sauté onion in butter until golden; add to potato mixture and season with salt and pepper.
2. **Assemble the Tacos:** Warm tortillas, fill with pierogi filling, and top with sour cream and chives.
3. **Serve:** Enjoy!

Moroccan Harissa Veggie Tacos

Ingredients

For the Veggie Filling:

- 1 zucchini, diced
- 1 bell pepper, diced
- 1 carrot, shredded
- 2 tbsp harissa paste
- 1 can (15 oz) chickpeas, drained
- Salt and pepper to taste

For the Tacos:

- 8 small tortillas
- Feta cheese, crumbled
- Fresh mint leaves

Instructions

1. **Cook the Veggies:** In a skillet, heat oil over medium heat. Add zucchini, bell pepper, and carrot; sauté until tender. Stir in chickpeas and harissa; cook for an additional 5 minutes. Season with salt and pepper.
2. **Assemble the Tacos:** Warm tortillas, fill with veggie mixture, and top with feta and mint.
3. **Serve:** Enjoy!

Egyptian Koshari Tacos

Ingredients

For the Koshari Filling:

- 1 cup cooked lentils
- 1 cup cooked rice
- 1 cup cooked macaroni
- 1 onion, sliced
- 2 cloves garlic, minced
- 1 can (14 oz) diced tomatoes
- 1 tsp cumin
- Salt and pepper to taste

For the Tacos:

- 8 small tortillas
- Spicy tomato sauce
- Chopped parsley

Instructions

1. **Prepare the Koshari:** In a skillet, heat oil and sauté onion and garlic until golden. Add diced tomatoes, cumin, salt, and pepper; simmer for 10 minutes. Stir in lentils, rice, and macaroni.
2. **Assemble the Tacos:** Warm tortillas, fill with koshari mixture, and drizzle with spicy tomato sauce.
3. **Serve:** Enjoy!

Korean Kimchi Pork Belly Tacos

Ingredients

For the Pork Belly Filling:

- 1 lb (450g) pork belly, sliced
- 1 cup kimchi, chopped
- 2 tbsp soy sauce
- 1 tbsp sesame oil
- 1 tbsp sugar

For the Tacos:

- 8 small tortillas
- Sliced green onions
- Sesame seeds

Instructions

1. **Cook the Pork Belly:** In a skillet, cook pork belly over medium heat until crispy. Add kimchi, soy sauce, sesame oil, and sugar; stir and cook until heated through.
2. **Assemble the Tacos:** Warm tortillas, fill with kimchi pork belly, and top with green onions and sesame seeds.
3. **Serve:** Enjoy!

Mexican Al Pastor Tacos

Ingredients

For the Al Pastor Filling:

- 1 lb (450g) pork shoulder, thinly sliced
- 2 tbsp achiote paste
- 1/4 cup pineapple juice
- 1/2 onion, chopped
- 2 cloves garlic, minced
- Salt to taste

For the Tacos:

- 8 small tortillas
- Diced pineapple
- Chopped cilantro
- Lime wedges

Instructions

1. **Marinate the Pork:** In a bowl, mix achiote paste, pineapple juice, onion, garlic, and salt. Add pork and marinate for at least 1 hour.
2. **Cook the Pork:** In a skillet, cook marinated pork until browned and cooked through.
3. **Assemble the Tacos:** Warm tortillas, fill with al pastor, and top with pineapple and cilantro. Serve with lime wedges.
4. **Serve:** Enjoy!

Dominican Mangu Tacos

Ingredients

For the Mangu Filling:

- 2 green plantains, peeled and sliced
- 1/2 cup onion, sliced
- 2 tbsp butter
- 1/2 cup vegetable broth
- Salt to taste

For the Tacos:

- 8 small tortillas
- Sliced avocado
- Pickled red onions

Instructions

1. **Prepare the Mangu:** Boil plantains until tender. Mash with butter, broth, and salt until smooth.
2. **Sauté the Onions:** In a skillet, sauté onions until caramelized.
3. **Assemble the Tacos:** Warm tortillas, fill with mangu, top with avocado, and pickled onions.
4. **Serve:** Enjoy!

Venezuelan Arepa Tacos

Ingredients

For the Arepa Filling:

- 2 cups arepa flour
- 2 cups water
- 1 cup shredded cheese (queso blanco)
- 1 cup shredded cooked chicken
- Salt to taste

For the Tacos:

- 8 small tortillas
- Sliced avocado
- Hot sauce

Instructions

1. **Make the Arepa Dough:** Mix arepa flour, water, and salt; form into small patties.
2. **Cook the Arepas:** Cook arepas on a griddle until golden on both sides.
3. **Assemble the Tacos:** Warm tortillas, fill with cheese, chicken, and top with avocado and hot sauce.
4. **Serve:** Enjoy!

Thai Green Curry Fish Tacos

Ingredients

For the Fish Filling:

- 1 lb (450g) white fish fillets (like cod or tilapia)
- 2 tbsp green curry paste
- 1 can (14 oz) coconut milk
- 1 tbsp fish sauce
- Juice of 1 lime
- Fresh basil leaves, for garnish

For the Tacos:

- 8 small tortillas
- Sliced cucumber
- Shredded carrots

Instructions

1. **Cook the Fish:** In a skillet, combine coconut milk, green curry paste, fish sauce, and lime juice. Bring to a simmer and add fish fillets. Cook until fish is flaky, about 5-7 minutes.
2. **Assemble the Tacos:** Warm tortillas, fill with green curry fish, and top with cucumber and carrots. Garnish with fresh basil.
3. **Serve:** Enjoy!

Italian Caprese Tacos

Ingredients

For the Caprese Filling:

- 2 cups cherry tomatoes, halved
- 1 cup fresh mozzarella balls, halved
- 1/2 cup fresh basil, chopped
- 2 tbsp balsamic glaze
- Salt and pepper to taste

For the Tacos:

- 8 small tortillas

Instructions

1. **Prepare the Filling:** In a bowl, combine cherry tomatoes, mozzarella, basil, balsamic glaze, salt, and pepper.
2. **Assemble the Tacos:** Warm tortillas and fill with Caprese mixture.
3. **Serve:** Enjoy!

Indian Tandoori Paneer Tacos

Ingredients

For the Paneer Filling:

- 1 lb (450g) paneer, cubed
- 1/2 cup plain yogurt
- 2 tbsp tandoori masala
- 1 tbsp lemon juice
- Salt to taste

For the Tacos:

- 8 small tortillas
- Sliced red onion
- Chopped cilantro

Instructions

1. **Marinate the Paneer:** In a bowl, mix yogurt, tandoori masala, lemon juice, and salt. Add paneer and marinate for at least 30 minutes.
2. **Cook the Paneer:** Grill or pan-fry the marinated paneer until golden.
3. **Assemble the Tacos:** Warm tortillas, fill with tandoori paneer, and top with red onion and cilantro.
4. **Serve:** Enjoy!

Pakistani Nihari Beef Tacos

Ingredients

For the Nihari Filling:

- 1 lb (450g) beef shank, cut into chunks
- 2 tbsp nihari spice mix
- 1 onion, chopped
- 4 cups beef broth
- 2 tbsp ginger-garlic paste
- Salt to taste

For the Tacos:

- 8 small tortillas
- Sliced ginger
- Chopped cilantro

Instructions

1. **Cook the Nihari:** In a pot, sauté onion and ginger-garlic paste until fragrant. Add beef, nihari spice mix, and broth; simmer for 2-3 hours until tender.
2. **Assemble the Tacos:** Warm tortillas, fill with nihari beef, and top with sliced ginger and cilantro.
3. **Serve:** Enjoy!

Colombian Ajiaco Chicken Tacos

Ingredients

For the Ajiaco Filling:

- 1 lb (450g) chicken breasts
- 2 potatoes, diced
- 1 corn on the cob, cut into rounds
- 1/2 cup guascas (dried herb)
- Salt and pepper to taste

For the Tacos:

- 8 small tortillas
- Sliced avocado
- Sour cream

Instructions

1. **Prepare the Ajiaco:** In a pot, boil chicken, potatoes, corn, guascas, salt, and pepper until cooked through. Shred chicken and mix well.
2. **Assemble the Tacos:** Warm tortillas, fill with ajiaco filling, and top with avocado and sour cream.
3. **Serve:** Enjoy!

Singaporean Chili Crab Tacos

Ingredients

For the Crab Filling:

- 1 lb (450g) cooked crab meat
- 1/2 cup chili crab sauce
- 1 tbsp soy sauce
- 1 tsp sesame oil
- Chopped green onions, for garnish

For the Tacos:

- 8 small tortillas
- Sliced cucumbers

Instructions

1. **Prepare the Crab Filling:** In a bowl, mix crab meat, chili crab sauce, soy sauce, and sesame oil.
2. **Assemble the Tacos:** Warm tortillas, fill with chili crab mixture, and top with cucumbers and green onions.
3. **Serve:** Enjoy!